A Letter for Daria

A Letter for Daria

BY EKATERINA GORDEEVA

WITH ANTONINA W. BOUIS

Little, Brown and Company
BOSTON NEW YORK TORONTO LONDON

Also by Ekaterina Gordeeva
My Sergei

⊶ ▰◆▰ ⊷

Title page photograph and chapter opener photographs
by Dana Finemann/SYGMA

ISBN 0-316-32994-0

Published simultaneously in Canada
by Little, Brown & Company (Canada) Limited

Printed in the United States of America

A Letter for Daria

$\mathcal{O}$nce upon a time, there was a little girl named Daria. She had two houses. One was in Connecticut, where she lived with her mother and her grandparents. She called it her "regular house." And one, which she called the "dacha" or "summer house," was in Russia. Daria went to the dacha in the summer with her family.

At her regular house, Daria had friends and toys and school. At her dacha, Daria had friends and toys and the woods and meadows.

One day, Daria wanted to pick mushrooms. So she got on a plane and flew to the dacha. She found a very, very big mushroom. And then she went to the airport, got on another plane, and brought the mushroom home.

Daria never got tired, because she could sleep in the plane.

Whichever house she was in, her family was with her. Daria loved both houses, because both were home.

Daria, my little Dasha, I am writing this book for you. I hope it will bring a smile more than once when you learn to read it by yourself. You are my daughter, my baby, the dearest person in the world to me. You are flesh of my flesh. And yet there are so many differences between us: I was born in Russia, and you were born in America; I had to study hard to learn English, and for you it's like a second native tongue. A whole new world is opening up for you through English. And you are opening up America for me, a country I might never had gotten to know well if not for you.

For instance, I had never heard of Mother's Day.

You'll learn as you get older that women are treated differently in Russia and in America. In Russia we celebrated March 8, International Women's Day. It was supposed to mark the solidarity of working women of the world. It was a real surprise for me when I realized that no one in America had ever heard of it—wasn't it supposed to be "international"? On that day, all women, whether they're mothers or not, get flowers. We used to make cards for our mothers at school. We would draw stems and leaves on poster paper and then glue on puffs of cotton, which we would then color, to make little yellow mimosas. My father would give my mother flowers and perfume.

But since International Women's Day is not celebrated here, I was completely overwhelmed when you came home one day in May with a present for me. You had worked on a big red heart with a friend, and on it was written *I Love Mommy* in English. "I love you, too," I replied in Russian.

HOME IN AMERICA

"I'm a Russian girl. And I'm an American girl. I'm both."

$\mathcal{A}$merica is your home. And mine. And your grandparents' home, too. We love it here. But I want you to also love my Russia, the place where I spent my happiest years—my childhood—and where I grew up and trained to be a figure skater. It was skating that brought your father and me to America. But it was you who made us decide to settle here.

Let me tell you how you, a little Russian girl, ended up being born in America. Your father and I were Russian figure skating stars, and we had traveled the world over. Ice palaces in many countries gave us a warm welcome. But we liked it best in the United States. We had friends and colleagues here. And when it came time for you to be born, we decided that it would be best for everyone—for you, for me, for the whole family that was eagerly awaiting you—if you were born in America. We knew that you and I would have the best medical care here.

One of my favorite stories that your grandmother Alyona tells is about how you were born a few days earlier than expected, on a Friday, and how she couldn't get here from Moscow until Monday. Then she waited nervously at the airport for five hours before your father picked her up. He was so excited that he couldn't concentrate enough to figure out how to pull up at the terminal, and he kept driving around and around the airport! She arrived at our house in the evening, and I led her to the room where you were in your little crib.

"Just don't be mad at me," I said, lifting up a corner of your blanket and showing you to her. "Look at what we got."

You were so tiny and wrinkled and hairless, and I didn't know if you were supposed to look like that or not.

A Letter for Daria

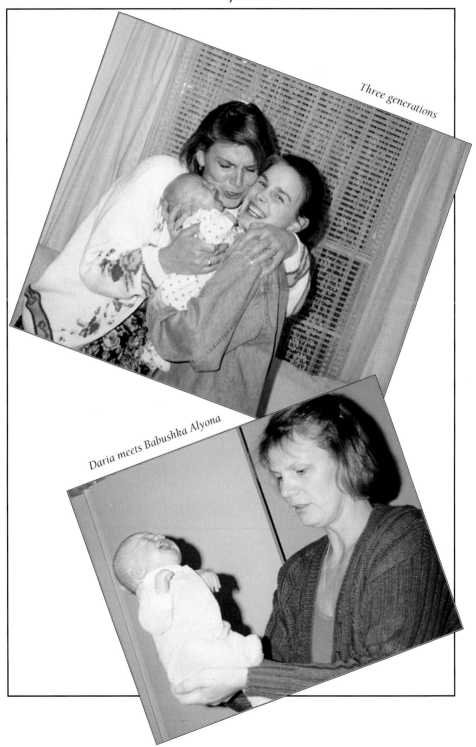

Three generations

Daria meets Babushka Alyona

Your grandmother laughed. "You should have seen yourself when you were a newborn. She's a miracle! She's perfect!"

You were a miracle from the start.

You know that almost none of the skating stars have babies. Most of them don't even have a real home, much less children, because they are on the road so much. You were the miracle that created a home for us. Everything became centered around you: we bought a house, and we brought over my parents to live with us and to be with you when we had to travel.

Most professional skaters live out of a suitcase. We travel, train, and do our show. And we put off having a baby, because that means having to stop skating for a year. And then getting back into shape. So instead, we skate more and get better. And the better we get, the better are the offers made to us. And the harder they are to refuse.

And that cycle is a trap that leaves no time for a personal life.

Sergei and Daria

That's why I thank God for the miracle that is you. And with every passing year, I appreciate you more and more. You are a piece of Sergei, your father. I am so glad we had you. He is gone, but you are with me.

We didn't plan on having you. I don't know when we would have picked the "right" time. It just happened. Sergei, my parents, and Father Nikolai, who married us, all supported me in the decision to have you. And thanks to you, I have a reason for living and for thinking of the future.

Your father and I called you Daria, because I remembered my mother always saying that if she had had a third daughter after my little sister, Masha, she would have called her Daria. I've always liked the name. We had a name for a boy picked out, too. Either Yegor—a good Russian name—or Mikhail, for Sergei's father.

And you know, we had no idea that you would automatically become an American citizen by being born here. We didn't know about that law. You can decide about your passport when you're eighteen. But I want you to remember your Russian roots. I love this country—the warm and friendly people, our wonderful new house. But if you were to wake me up in the middle of the night and ask me what I am, I'd reply, "Russian." I don't think I'll ever be able to become a real American. I was born in Russia, and everyone in my family is Russian. You can become an American, though. And I think you will.

America is a very generous, welcoming place. You can "become" American, in a way that you couldn't "become" Japanese or Swedish or French. And you can still treasure your heritage and be proud of it, because it enriches your new country. You can love both countries. I certainly do.

It's very strange: I feel as if I've had two lives. The first is my Russian life, the one when I was little. I had a long and marvelous childhood and adolescence, in which I trained and skated with Sergei. The second is

A Letter for Daria

Sergei, Katia, and Daria in Moscow

the one I'm living now, in America. Sometimes it feels as if I live in Russia and work in America. That maybe when I stop working, when my career is over, I'll go back home. My home is here now with you, but my hometown is still Moscow. I'm very happy that I have

Sergei, Katia, and Daria

two homes; I don't consider one better than the other. I have family and friends here, and I have family and friends there.

I'm glad that I don't have to cut the thread that connects us to Russia. Times have changed, and people are no longer forced to choose — to either live in the Soviet Union or leave and never go back. You are so lucky — you'll have a double vision of life, through American and Russian eyes, and you will be the richer for it.

I'm very happy in America, but it's in Russia that I feel truly relaxed and like a child again. When I'm on Russian soil, I know that wherever I set foot I'm at home, whatever I do is all right.

Even before you were born, your father and I were already spending half the year in America and half in Russia. We didn't have a home; we were like gypsies. "A person is a guest in life," someone said. When America welcomed us, we felt we had to prove that we were good guests and earn our place at the table.

It's not an easy thing to do, but we were lucky, because figure skating is very popular in America. I am grateful to my profession. If I had been a singer who sang in Russian, I would not have found the understanding audience I have. The language of movement does not need translation.

Figure skating is special because it is both a sport and an art. Once you've won your Olympic medals, you can prolong your career by going professional. You keep on working, learning how to build onto what you've learned before. You move from pure sport to showmanship and artistry.

Russia is the best country for training athletes and performers. But America is the best place for us to have the freedom to grow artistically and to be appreciated by audiences.

STARS ON ICE

*"My mama is only one of the stars.
They're all stars, silly."*

 $\mathcal{I}$ 'm so happy that your father and I joined Stars on Ice; it led to our settling down in Simsbury, Connecticut. The people in the show have become our friends, and they all get such a kick out of you.

What I like is your attitude toward them and toward my work. A friend told me that she asked you if you were proud that your mother was a star, the star of the show. She thought putting it that way would make you feel important. Instead, you corrected her.

You replied, "My mama's only one of the stars. They're all stars, silly. That's why it's called Stars on Ice."

I hope you keep that objectivity and balance throughout your life. Don't be impressed by things that are not important. Being a star is not important (though it is fun). What is important is doing your very best.

I can't tell you what that nervous tension is like when you come out into the crossed spotlights on the ice and know that millions of people all over the world are watching you on television, waiting for you to give them pleasure.

You have to do your best. It's hard work. And it's worth it. But when I know that you're in the audience, I have a special glow. I forget about everyone else. I know that you're sitting there in the stands behind me and that when I skate past, I can give you a special smile—our own little secret. And it's wonderful to hear you say after the show, "Mama, you were so beautiful today."

You've picked up the travel bug yourself. When you were just two, you asked, "When will we go to the airport?" Or you'd say, "Mama, we've been in this hotel long enough. Two whole days! Isn't it time to go to the next city?" You've ridden on the Barney Bus (Why do we call it that? Because it's the color of Barney the Dinosaur!) with the cast of Stars on Ice as we go from one town to the next.

You've flown to a lot of cities in America. At first your father and I took you with us because we had no place to leave you, since we didn't have a home in the U.S. That was hard on us all. So was leaving you in Moscow with my parents. Buying the house in Connecticut and bringing my mother and father to stay with you there while we were on tour was the perfect solution.

Now you have two homes, and you commute between them by airplane. There's the house in America and the dacha, the summer house, in Russia.

Your grandmother brings you to visit when I'm on tour for a long time. I'm amazed that you remember so much. "Mama, we've been in this hotel before. Remember?" "Hear that music? Scott danced to it in the show." "Kristi's best costume is the daisy flower one." Often, these are things that you saw more than a year earlier.

Since I'm the only member of the show with a child, you cheer up everyone, not just me, when you come to visit. You brighten up the long, lonely hotel corridors as you scoot along, visiting everyone's rooms. When we've been on the road for a while, it's really great to have a cuddly, laughing Daria to take our minds off the bus, the food, the airports, the hotels. When you're older, I'll take you to the opera to see *The Daughter of the Regiment*. That's who you are for us.

I think all the skaters have a special smile for you when you're in the audience. But our special secret smile is just for us alone.

For Mommy

MY BABUSHKA

"Babushkas know everything."

$\mathcal{D}$o you want to know another secret? I would not have become a skating star without my darling grandmother. You know the Russian word for grandmother—it's *babushka,* pronounced with the accent on the first syllable: BAH-boosh-kah. It's Russia's real secret weapon. Without babushkas, families would fall apart.

I started on the ice when I was four. I don't remember my first time, but I must have enjoyed it and been good at it, because I continued. Since I was a tiny little girl, the coach encouraged me. The boys needed partners they could lift easily.

I also went to a dance group for a while. My father, Alexander, was a dancer, and he wanted me to dance, but I liked skating better. Maybe because I was better at it. Maybe because I liked the skating choreography teacher better than the dancing teacher. The teacher is so important.

You probably remember how we took you to try gymnastics and rhythmic gymnastics. Your American gym teachers were a lot of fun and made the experience enjoyable right away. They let you try out all the equipment, the balance beam, the rings. The rhythmic gymnastics teachers were from Russia, and they started you on stretching exercises. It hurt so much that you refused to go back.

That's when I realized how much will power and determination have to come from the parents or grandparents when children take sports. I didn't have the strength to force you to go back after you had been hurt. I tried to explain to you that you had to put up with some pain in order to get better, in order to become beautiful. You seemed to understand and agree with my reasoning, but there was no way that you would go there again.

Even though I loved skating, there were times my babushka had to persuade me to go back after a hard workout at the rink. She knew that I fell on the cold ice, that I got bruised sometimes, that I felt frustrated when I couldn't master a jump or a turn right away. Sometimes the coach hurt my feelings. Sometimes I wanted to eat something that wasn't on my diet.

But she was always there for me. Soothing. Consoling. Encouraging. "I know it hurts. But it will get better, and you will be beautiful." "I know you want dessert. Tonight you can't have any. But tomorrow you can. And look what I cooked specially for you tonight." "I know the coach was mean today. But he'll be nice tomorrow."

And it wasn't only the emotional support that she gave me. She also gave me the time. She took me to the rink for early morning practice. She took me after school. She could do what my parents couldn't do. They had to go to work; they would come home tired. Babushka was devoted to me. And she kept the house running, too.

We all had our jobs. My job, according to my father, was skating. And that made me very proud. I was proud of my mother when she went to her job, all dressed up and looking pretty. She was important. I loved watching her get ready in the morning. And I loved waiting for her to return at night. She worked for the Soviet press agency, TASS, and sometimes she traveled. I loved her postcards, but it was always a great moment when she came home.

My father traveled for work, too. He was a dancer with the Alexandrov Dance Ensemble, and they performed all over the world. In those days, Soviet citizens were not allowed to have a lot of foreign currency, so in order to save money, my father would not eat in restaurants in all those countries. He would take a lot of food with him. I remember my mother packing salamis, canned meat and fish, crackers, cookies, a small teakettle, tea, and sugar. He went off with his suitcases full of food, and he came back with suitcases full of presents for us.

He would be away for months at a time. So we sent him letters and drawings. My sister and I would go to a photographer's studio to have pictures taken of us for him. And my mother would be busy at her office. So naturally, we all depended on Babushka.

A Letter for Daria

As I said, I tried to talk to you about rhythmic gymnastics the way she used to talk to me about skating, about being patient and putting up with the pain. I told you that stretching hurts, that it hurts me when I do it, but it's worth it. You would be beautiful. You would have a beautiful costume and perform in a beautiful show.

You said you understood. But when it was time to go back, you screamed and wouldn't budge. I couldn't force you. I remembered when my sister, Masha, tried figure skating. She's four years younger than I am. After her first time at the rink, she declared that she would never return. "Your hands get cold when you fall on the ice, and they don't let you eat," she said. She never went back.

More and more I realize that my success depended totally on my grandmother. I'm one hundred percent certain that if I hadn't had a babushka like that, I would not have achieved anything as a skater. She was always there for me. Her career being a babushka. And she was as much a star in her field as I am in mine.

THE DACHA

"God gives you the things that you can't buy with money, like babushkas and sunshine."

$\mathcal{I}$ remember only one time that I made a fuss about having to practice. It was the first September after I started school, when my parents told me it was time to leave the dacha, the summer house, and go back to school and the rink. I didn't want to go back to Moscow! Not to school and not on the ice. I wanted it to be summer forever.

Summer was the best time, and the dacha was the best place in the world. My grandparents rented half a dacha, and I spent the whole summer there with them. My parents would come out on weekends. They slept up in the attic. I can picture every corner of the house, especially the terrace, which I loved so much. When I shut my eyes, I can see every tree, every path, every flower. We had everything there. I could play outside with the other kids. I was in love with one of the boys. When Masha got bigger, she and I had a tent in the yard. My grandfather took me fishing with the special kid-size pole he made for me. One day he promised me we would catch a huge pike. We caught a frog and left it on the line overnight. In the morning, we went down to the river, and there it was, a huge fish that we could barely haul onto shore.

I didn't like swimming in the river, because there were leeches and I was afraid of them. In fact, swimming is one sport that I'm not very good at and don't particularly like. Not like you! You love the pool. You would go every day with your babushka if you could. You have no fear of the water at all—you dive off the board gleefully and hurry to line up for another turn. Why, even your favorite story is "The Little Mermaid."

Your grandmother is an excellent swimmer. On some of our vacations, my parents would take us to the

Black Sea. We'd drive for three days from Moscow until we got to the coast, somewhere near Sochi. I remember watching her swim way out far and worrying that the sea would swallow her up.

Do you know what happened one day at the beach? I lost my sister, Masha. It was one of the scariest things that ever happened to me. She and I were digging in the sand, building castles, and my mother said, "Papa and I are going to lie down right there near the water. You keep an eye on your sister." We were busily digging away, when Masha said she wanted to go to Mama. I pointed to my parents, just a few feet away in a straight line from us, and said, "Do you see them over there? Just go straight to them." And kept on digging.

A little while later, Mama came over, looked at my castle, and then said, "Where's Masha?"

"What do you mean? She's with you."

"No, she's not."

You can imagine how scared I got. My parents separated, one going left along the beach, the other right, looking everywhere for Masha. My mother kept describing her and asking if anyone had seen her. At last, a woman told her that she had seen a gypsy woman with a little girl like that. Gypsies sold candy and fruit at the beach. And sure enough, my mother ran and caught up with the woman, who was holding Masha in her arms.

I felt terrible. It was my responsibility to watch over my little sister, and I had let her wander off. Thank God, nothing had happened to her. My parents didn't even yell at me. They could see how awful I felt.

After our vacation trips with our parents, Masha and I went back to the dacha for the rest of the summer. I actually like the woods and mountains more than the beach. I prefer the weather to be on the cool side. And I like the shady paths of the forest.

Grandfather told me stories when we were in the woods, and he taught me how to look for mushrooms. Different kinds grow under different trees, you know. And you have to be very careful not to pick poisonous ones. You have to hunt mushrooms with an expert.

How I loved summer at the dacha! There were lightning bugs and ladybugs. There were bunnies and turtles and hedgehogs, sunsets and sunrises, wind and sun, stars and moon, a river and a pond. I could do whatever I wanted.

I've taken you there. Remember, when you were three, we went looking for mushrooms, and even though it was only June, too early in the season, we managed to find quite a few. I wish my grandfather could have seen you!

You immediately made friends with a local girl and invented all kinds of games. You called me over to cover a big box you were playing in, so that no one would know that you two had a secret playhouse in there. It reminded me of the games I played with Masha.

We also liked to put on shows. Since I was the big sister, I got to boss her around. I would be the director and choreographer and star, and she would have to keep doing her part over and over until I was satisfied. We sang and danced and made up stories.

The happiest times I ever had were at the dacha, and even now when I think about Russia, it's the dacha I think about first.

Of course, summer did come to an end, and we did move back to the city. My life was perfectly happy and ordinary.

I paid little attention to politics and to the names of the country's rulers. But I certainly noticed when Gorbachev came to power. Moscow changed — there were fewer red flags, more signs and ads, more imported food and clothing. My mother traveled more. I guess TASS was covering Gorbachev's travels. The next time the Olympics came around, I was a member of the team and even went to a banquet at the Kremlin hosted by Gorbachev!

And all that was thanks to Babushka's patience with me.

Your Babushka

"I wish I could swim in the pool all day with Babushka. And breathe under water like a mermaid."

$\mathcal{B}$ut somehow in America, there are no babushkas. Grandparents often live in cities far away and see their grandchildren only on holidays. I think that's a mistake. It's good to be around your grandchildren. They give you energy and keep you young. I can see how my parents age (and they're only pushing fifty) when they're not with you. I'm glad that we've managed to preserve the Russian tradition of an extended family even in America and that you have your own babushka with you.

I was very lucky—my babushka was great. You

are even luckier when it comes to grandmothers. My mother, whose pet name in the family is Alyona, is unique, my best friend, the center of our family. She was born to be a diplomat. There is no one with whom she cannot get along. And she makes sure that all our family members get along. My father can be difficult, and, I'm afraid, so can I. I take after him. But my mother holds us all together like a magnet of love and energy.

When I faced the very difficult task of keeping up my career and having a baby, my mother saved the day. She quit her job and took on my family, so that I could go on training and traveling. She made it so easy for your father and me. And I don't know what I would have done, how I could have gone on without her when your father died. She is the source of my strength. She is the one who made me realize that I had to go on for your sake. And for my own.

She has an incredible quality: she gives advice only when you ask for it. And she never forces her opinion on you. She listens and somehow—this is the part I don't understand but appreciate—as she listens,

you come to a decision on your own, although it's the very thing she would have chosen.

I always turn to my mother first when I have a problem. Before I talk to friends. Usually, it's because she has experience. For instance, if you're sick, I call her to find out what she used to give me when I had the same thing. She tells me, but she also reminds me that I should talk to your doctor first.

Alyona has only one rule that cannot be broken: stay in touch. Call when you're out. Call to say when you'll be back. Call if you're running late. That applies to everyone, including my father. It's not a rule for children who can't be trusted; it's a rule for people who care about others and do not want to cause unnecessary worry. Stay in touch.

The other thing we learned was not to lie, not to cover up. To this day, it's the worst sin as far as I'm concerned: lying, hiding, twisting the truth, saying one thing and doing another. And I'm teaching you this, too—to tell the truth. To confess if you've done something wrong—even if you know you'll be in trouble and will be punished. I always felt worse during the time that I kept a guilty secret from my mother than when I finally told and got punished. The guilt was a worse punishment.

My mother permitted everything else. She felt that I would persist until I tried whatever it was I wanted to do. Then we could talk about it to decide whether it was a good thing or a bad one. For instance, I would ask to do something silly, like wear shoes instead of boots out in the snow (just as you do now, by the way). She would tell me no once, twice, and finally say, "All right. I guess you have to get your feet cold and wet and come down with a cold before you believe me."

And she was that way about almost everything. A child needs to see for herself. I have this same problem with you now. You can't understand why you need to wear boots if there's frost on the grass. You don't understand why I say no. Children don't understand about consequences, about future results of actions. But I am different from your babushka. I put your boots on you and agree that they are not as pretty as your shoes and tell you that you can take them off the minute you get to school, before anyone sees them, and change into your pretty shoes.

My mother's method of letting us learn the hard way didn't apply to the truly serious problems, like sex and alcohol, because she made a point of discussing things with me before they came up. She liked to talk about things at a time when they weren't an issue, when it wasn't a crisis, so that they could be discussed calmly. She was always talking to us, making us look at our behavior. She wouldn't say, this is bad or this is wrong. Instead, she would bring up examples of ways to react, for instance, what she would have done in that situation, and ask, "What do you think? Which is better?" Sometimes my father grumbled that there was too much talk.

Alyona learned that approach from her own mother, who always talked to her about everything under the sun. "She explained everything ten times over. Constantly. While she was making soup for me, she would talk about life, moral choices, without reference to anything in particular." That's how your babushka learned from mine.

My parents would say to me, "All right. Let us tell you our opinion. You can do what you want. But hear us out." That was their way of helping me develop my independence.

You see how we pass ideas and traditions from generation to generation. I suppose you'll have no trouble guessing who brought up your grandmother Alyona. That's right, her grandmother. Alyona's father was an army officer and taught at the military academy, training young officers. Alyona's mother, my babushka, ran the house and took care of her husband. She made sure that he was not bothered by any household details. Being an officer's wife involved many social events and a lot of travel. They lived in Bulgaria for a while, where he was organizing a military academy. She was very busy.

So when your grandmother was a little girl, she spent a lot of time with her father's mother, her babushka Mania. She took Alyona for walks and to dance class. She also supervised her lessons in English and music.

It's good that Alyona studied all these things when

she was a little girl. I don't think she would have been able to without her grandmother's time and effort. And look what happened: the English certainly came in handy, although I'm sure Alyona never dreamed that one day she would be living in Connecticut. And the dancing lessons led to true love. Alyona met Alexander in a dance ensemble when they were teenagers. Even though they never danced with each other onstage, they got to know each other and fell in love.

They got married when they were still teenagers. I was born when my mother was twenty. Masha came four years later. We all lived together with my mother's parents.

We had a large apartment in Moscow. There was Grandfather's room, Babushka's room, my parents' room, and the room I shared with my sister. When our homework was finished, we were allowed to watch cartoons. In those days, we didn't have a cartoon channel or a VCR. So we eagerly waited for the time that the show would be on. We couldn't play it over and over the way you do with your favorite Disney movies. Sometimes I catch you watching TV and staring at it so hard your eyes are watering. "Don't forget to blink!" I have to remind you. You soak up information like a sponge—when you watch TV, you're learning about America and learning new English words.

My favorite holiday was New Year's. In Soviet Russia, where Christmas was not officially celebrated because religion was banned, they turned New Year's into a secular children's holiday, using many of the Christmas traditions. There was a tree with lights and ornaments, presents, and even the Russian Santa Claus, Grandfather Frost.

At our house, we had a big sack of presents under the tree, and it was so exciting to reach into the sack and pull out gifts. For Masha! For Grandfather! For Katia! For Mama! The best present I ever got was a toy telephone that actually worked. Masha had a receiver in one room, and I had the other one in another room. And we could talk to each other. I remember it to this day.

There was never any problem about bedtime for me—I was usually exhausted and ready to jump into bed. My mother or my babushka would read to me.

My father made lots of rules. We had to keep our room very neat. We had to have our homework done on time and perfectly. They were the usual rules most parents have for their children, but in our family, he was the one who made them.

My father was a perfectionist. If I had a blotch in my copybook, a cross-out in my homework, he made me do it over. He made me so nervous when he checked my homework that I couldn't even handle simple problems if he tried to explain something to me. So I usually waited for my mother to come home and had her look at my work.

She would go over my homework with me patiently and calmly. Your babushka made it so easy for my sister and me to meet our obligations at school and at home. She encouraged us with a smile and rewarded us the same way.

A Letter for Daria

Daria with Dyeda
Alexander

SKATING

"I saw a real mermaid once, in Disney World. I'd like to be a mermaid, but then I wouldn't have any feet and I couldn't skate with Mama."

$\mathcal{M}$y father's perfectionism extended to my skating, of course. He made me do things ten times if the coach said do it five. He demanded perfection from me, and I learned from him to demand it of myself. I found it difficult living up to his standards, but now I realize that he faced the same demands with his dancing and they made him demanding with himself and with us.

However, he's not that way with you. He wants you to keep your room neat, but if you don't clean it up by yourself, he helps you. He never helped us. He's really mellowed, so you get the best of him. All his good points and none of his bad.

I find myself being as demanding as he used to be. It's very hard to remember that people make mistakes, that people can have moods. I keep reminding myself that it is important to forgive imperfection, the way your grandmother does. But on the other hand, it was my father's perfectionism that pushed me to push myself.

My mother thinks I overdo it. "Why don't you give yourself a break?" she asks. I find it very hard to do nothing. So, just as I had to force myself to overcome my laziness and accomplish things when I was a teenager, now I have to force myself to relax.

It's very hard to break the habits of a lifetime. I have to stay in shape, in peak condition. My body is my instrument. It demands constant attention. I have to watch what I eat. I have to practice and train. I have to rest before a performance. I'm the only one who can control those things. I have to take complete responsibility for my life and my body. That doesn't leave me much time for other things. That's why it's so wonderful that my mother is able to devote time to you. I can't spend hours at your gymnastics class or at the pool with you, because I have to be doing my own training. I can't take you to school every day, because I spend weeks traveling with the tour. But your babushka can take you. She can watch you swim or do gymnastics, bring you home, and give you a cozy meal. And read you a cozy story. Just the way my babushka did for me.

It's very important for children to do sports. It builds self-confidence, knowing that you can control your body. It keeps you from being awkward and clumsy. It's healthy. And for very small children, it's a way of developing discipline. When a coach tells you to sit and watch another little girl trying out something, you do it. It is easier to obey a coach than a teacher in a classroom situation. I think it is less stressful. You begin to learn what your body can do: you can balance on a beam, you can skate on the ice. There are people who have never tried to skate. That's like never trying to swim. Sports develop concentration and patience and other skills that apply to all aspects of life.

I train and stay in shape because I believe that you always have to do your personal best. Winning the gold is not the goal. The goal is to master the sport and to do it as well as you can. I worry when I hear young girls say that their dream is not to be a figure skater but to win a gold medal in the Olympics. Assuming they can and do, what then? If you achieve your life's goal when you're still a teenager, what is there to do for the next sixty years? It's very sad to contemplate a life without a goal to reach for. However, if you measure your achievements against your own personal accomplishments, you can continue perfecting your art for the rest of life.

A gold medal is simply the measure of one night's performance in comparison to the performance that

A Letter for Daria

same night of a few other people. It is not a lifetime achievement award. There are so many other factors involved. Our choreographer, Marina Zoueva, always told us that the judges are just people! They can be tired from the trip; they can be bored after watching a dozen other pairs before you. So you have to go out there and give them something different. Give them a smile. Cheer them up. That can influence your score, you know.

This may sound strange, but there were events early in our careers that had much more significance for Sergei and me than winning at the Olympics. When we were just starting out, winning was a much bigger step, a much harder accomplishment.

There is a lot of flag waving at the Olympic Games. Some people root for countries rather than athletes. But none of our coaches told us, "You're doing this for the Homeland!" or "Go

Dino Ricci

out there and win for the Soviet Union!" We had team spirit, and naturally, I felt that I was part of the Russian team. But my real team, *my* team, that was Sergei and I.

RELIGION

"In church you see pictures of God, but He's not there. You only see Him when you die."

$\mathcal{J}$ust the other morning, you'd been sleeping in my bed, and when you woke up, you turned to me and asked, "Where was I when Papa died? Why didn't I see it?" I explained that we had been up at Lake Placid, training, and that you weren't there. When he died, I tried to explain: I told you that his heart hurt and the doctors tried to help but couldn't do it. And you said, "That can happen to anyone—to a kitten or a bunny. The heart can hurt and then stop."

I know you are trying to understand it. Your teacher has been a big help; she's been with you through the whole experience. It's good to talk about it. The other day when we were reading "The Little Mermaid" again, at the part where it says that only human souls can go up to heaven and mermaids can't, you said, "See, that's like Papa. He lives in heaven. With the angels. But the little mermaid has to stay in the water and turn into foam."

When I was your age, I didn't know about angels or God. We didn't talk about it at home and certainly not at school. I had never been to church, and in fact I was a little afraid of them—they seemed so dark and gloomy. It was Sergei who took me to one for the first time. There were so many firsts with Sergei. Your father taught me so many things about life and love.

We were on tour in Europe, and whenever we had a few hours to see the city we were in, we'd end up looking at old churches. I never wanted to go inside. At last, he said, "Come on, look at the architecture, the stained glass windows, the carvings, the paintings. Light a candle. If you want something to happen, you light a candle."

He was right. It was beautiful. Once I became

aware of religion, I looked around more closely. Russians pray before icons—painted depictions of Christ or saints—in church and at home. And it turned out that my grandmother had an icon in her room. I had seen it many times, of course, but I just thought it was a painting of some handsome old man. It was a saint. She had a votive light, a small candle, next to it on a shelf, which she would sometimes light. I asked her about it, and she explained, "When I want everything to be good for you, I light it."

That's how religion began for me, with kindness, not with studying. I learned that God meant goodness and love.

When your father and I decided to get married, my mother said, "If you want a church wedding, you have to be baptized first." She had been baptized secretly, because religion was not allowed in the Soviet Union under the old Communist government. I knew nothing about it when I was growing up. And so I went to Father Nikolai's church to be christened. He is such a wonderful man. Father Nikolai prepared us for the state of holy matrimony. He understood my tentative faith. At the age of eighteen, I didn't know any prayers, but instead of making me feel guilty, he made me feel glad that I had found God.

When I looked back on my childhood, I realized that my grandmother had prayed, but I never asked her about it. I think it was out of respect for her privacy and her secret.

I go to church to pray sometimes, when I need to sort things out for myself. You can tell God the most secret deep feelings, what you can say only to yourself. But I don't like asking God for things all the time. You have to try to handle life by yourself first. Only when you've done your best can you turn for help and say, "Lord, help me, because I have done everything in my power and it is no longer up to me."

You go to church with me when we're in Moscow, to light a candle, to take communion. Father Nikolai and you get along so well. He has five children of his own. In the Russian church, priests are married so that they can better understand the cares of their parishioners. When we decided to have the Moscow apartment blessed, you helped Father Nikolai in the service, sprinkling holy water along with him in all directions.

I don't want to force religion on you. By exposing you to it, I hope that you will come to your own decision about it when you are old enough. You have a lot more than I did as a child—you've been baptized, you wear a cross, and you have a children's Bible to read at bedtime. Even without that, I made my way to religion when I was eighteen. When you are eighteen, you will have many decisions to make about your life—citizenship, college, religion. My goal is to prepare you so that you can make intelligent, informed decisions.

FAMILY TRAITS

"I'm a star, too."

$\mathcal{W}$e are all made up of pieces of our families. Parts of our psychology and personality come from our parents and grandparents. Some things we see and copy; others I believe we inherit.

There are traits that I hope you do inherit and some I sincerely hope you do not. But I already see a lot of familiar features in you.

Sergei was very confident in a positive way. I don't mean that he was conceited, far from it. But he was aware of his ability to handle a situation. For instance, when Marina, our choreographer, would come up with a new routine, I would rush to try out the steps. I knocked myself out on the ice, testing what I thought she wanted, while he just stood there thinking. He'd look at me, at her, at me, and then he'd do it once. "That's it!" Marina would cry. I'd be doing it a hundred times with no response; he'd make one movement once, and it would be perfect.

His approach was to think it through. First he watched and listened carefully. Unlike me. I start listening and then halfway through the explanation, I'm out there trying it out, even when I'm not sure what it is I'm supposed to be trying. He was just the opposite — Sergei had to comprehend and digest before he would do it.

You're the same way. You listen very attentively. Your teachers comment on that. I see it in the way you perform. Remember the movie we made for television? You were so professional when the director talked to you. He gave you instructions on how to act, and you did it without a problem. You had to pretend to fall asleep while I read to you. I wanted to rehearse the scene with you. You said, "Why practice? When it's time to do it, I'll do it."

Rosalynn Sumners

I said, "But, Dasha, you have to try things out."

"Don't worry, Mama. I'll do it right."

You yawned right on cue.

In another scene you had to pretend to get dizzy while skating and fall down onto the ice. Even I have to practice a fall. But you said, "No! I'll do it right when the director tells me to do it." Just like your father. I need to rehearse and practice. You two just do it right the first time.

You amazed me during the filming. When you arrived on the set, I worried that you weren't in costume yet. You said, "It's too early. Our scene is later." It never occurred to me to think about that. They told me to dress, and I got dressed. And stood there, waiting. You said, "Mama, take off your costume. What are you waiting for? The camera isn't set up over there."

I have an idea that you might end up in show business. You spend a lot of time around our show, backstage, around cameras and in front of them. You're good in the spotlight; you like the attention. I see it with your friends. You do something, and they follow you like little ducks. I don't know how you do it, but you're the leader. You have star quality. And you're serious and professional about the directions you're given.

That takes discipline and perseverance. I hope those are the traits you inherit from me. I've learned how it important it is to stick to it, no matter how hard or painful or boring it may be. The results are worth it.

But I don't want you going overboard and turning into a workaholic or perfectionist who demands too much of herself. Interestingly, my father doesn't push you the way he did me. Of course, you don't let him. He told me a funny story about a conversation the two of you had.

You said, "Grandfather, why are you always telling people what to do?"

"Repeat what you just said. What was the first word?" he countered.

"The first word was 'Grandfather.'"

"And that's why. I'm older and I know much more than you."

"Well, I can see why you teach me my alphabet," you replied. "But why do you think you can teach Mama how to skate?"

He does help you with your acting and dancing. He loves taking pictures of you, and often he'll tell you to express a feeling or to pretend to be doing something for the photograph. This past Halloween, you had a marvelous costume as a witch, with a black wig, pointy hat, and cape. He took a series of shots of you on a broom around the fireplace, looking as if you had just flown down the chimney.

Father encourages you to be neat and organized, which is great. So does your school. When you're playing at home and we call you to dinner, you say, "First it's Cleanup Time!" You put away toys and art supplies, dust your table, push in your chair, and wash your hands. That's the way you do it in school.

I hope you don't pick up my temper. I certainly don't mean to get upset over trifles, but sometimes I find myself unable to control my own words. Ten or fifteen minutes later, I'm so sorry, but it's too late. The words have been said; people's feelings have been hurt. I feel so bad when I get angry with you for spilling your milk or something. You're just a little girl, and accidents happen.

My mother doesn't get mad at you even if you

stamp your foot at her. She can distinguish between the action and the actor. She can say, "That's not nice." But she would never say, "You're not nice." She understands that there is a reason for behavior and that there must be a reason you are upset.

I certainly hope that you develop your babushka's talent for kindness, patience, and diplomacy. She has the energy to offer comfort whenever anyone needs it. Only she knows how to speak without hurting the feelings of anyone in the family, without judging or blaming. Even if I have been hurt by someone, she will focus on my pain and not on the other person's guilt.

She never criticizes anyone. Her theory is that she should not stop me from seeing people and dealing with people just because she does not like them. What matters is what I think of them. She would never say, "Don't have that girl come over to play—I don't like her" or "I think you shouldn't do business with him." She tolerates people for my sake without making an issue of it.

She will tell me her opinion if I ask. And I usually do because she doesn't force it on me. My mother's advice is balanced, generous, and nonjudgmental. When I'm away from her and have a problem, I try to imagine what she would do in my particular situation. If it fits with my own feelings, I follow that advice.

With your mix of family traits, you will have impulses to behave in different ways. You will also have several models to look back on and think, What would they do in this situation? When you face moments of decision later in life, I hope you will have the independence and courage (and I think you already do) to listen to your own feelings, draw on the best of your family memories, and make up your own mind.

Yuri Dojc

When You Grow Up

"I want to have a little girl. Her name will be Elizabeth."

As I write this book, I think about all that lies ahead for you. I have hopes and dreams for you, of course, and one special, secret wish.

I want you to have a full life, with time for everything. I regret not having studied more at school. I was too busy practicing at the rink to have more general interests in a wide variety of areas. I want you to know about physics and chemistry, history and art, mathematics and computers. Especially computers. They kind of scare me, because I don't know anything about them. You should not be afraid of anything.

Knowledge fights fear. The more you know, the more you'll want to learn.

I want you to be open to new experiences and to be prepared for whatever life brings. In your short life, you've already seen the best and worst. You lost your father, and you found out that family love and inner strength can help you deal with that loss.

For a while you picked up a manner of looking at his picture, shaking your little head, and clucking, "Poor, poor Papa!" That is not the way to remember him. I would say, "He's not poor at all! Look at him, look how happy he is! He had you, he had me, he was famous, and he had many friends! He looks like you — see, in this picture where he's holding you?"

You should hold on to the past, but only as a foundation for the future.

With a broad education, you will be able to decide what you want to be when you grow up. You have the whole world to choose from. The important thing to remember is that whatever you decide to do, you must do it to the best of your ability. The joy of achieving your personal best is a satisfaction that you can create for yourself no matter what your profession.

And you should make room in your life for things other than work.

I hope you'll play a musical instrument. I wish I could play even a few chords on a guitar. There's something so wonderful about a party where someone can play the guitar and people join in the singing.

You have other decisions to make, too. Somehow I think I know what choices you will make. You will choose American citizenship — how could you not, growing up in this wonderful country? I hope you will continue your relationship with God and the church.

You will fall in love. I think it will be someone you meet in college. I hope you get married early. It's a tradition in our family — look at your babushka and me.

I've imagined your wedding: it will be beautiful. A church wedding. The Russian ceremony is rather long but so lovely to see and hear. The ritual is mysterious and significant. It's full of symbolism and tradition. Friends of the bride and groom hold crowns over the couple's heads during the service. They do it in relays, usually three pairs of crown bearers, because it's hard holding a crown up that high for long. At one point the priest ties a white ribbon around the hands of the couple and leads them around a small altar three times, while the choir sings. The music is so beautiful—we have wonderful church choirs. Candles blaze, their smoke carrying prayers for the newlyweds' happiness up to the heavens. Afterward, the candles are saved as a memento of the wedding. The priest blesses the union, the bride and groom kiss, and then everyone congratulates them.

I can picture the wedding reception now. It will be outdoors in a beautiful location. Someplace as wonderful as our dacha. We'll have a striped tent in a meadow near water. There will be lots of food and drink. Russian and American. And music—also Russian and American. We'll sing and dance and celebrate the occasion all afternoon and well into the night.

You'll be a beautiful bride, and your husband will be strong, handsome, wise, and kind. You will love each other, enjoying every day to its fullest, accepting what life brings you. I've learned that you must savor every moment of life. It is precious, and it has meaning if you recognize that it does.

And here's my secret wish: that you give me grandchildren while I'm still young. Because I want to give your American children what you and I have been lucky enough to have: a Russian babushka.

*F*or at least three generations, the women in our family have learned from their grandmothers. It boils down to a few simple lessons. I hope you'll take them to heart:

BABUSHKA WISDOM

1. No rules.
2. No lies.
3. Call home.
4. Do what you have to do, and do it well.
5. Two gold medals do not equal one Dasha.
6. Parents are good; grandparents are great.
7. Home is where the heart is, but especially at the summer dacha.

"Babushka, you forgot two important rules:
Listen to your parents.
Eat all your food."

— Daria

A Letter for Daria

Daria, Alyona, and Katia

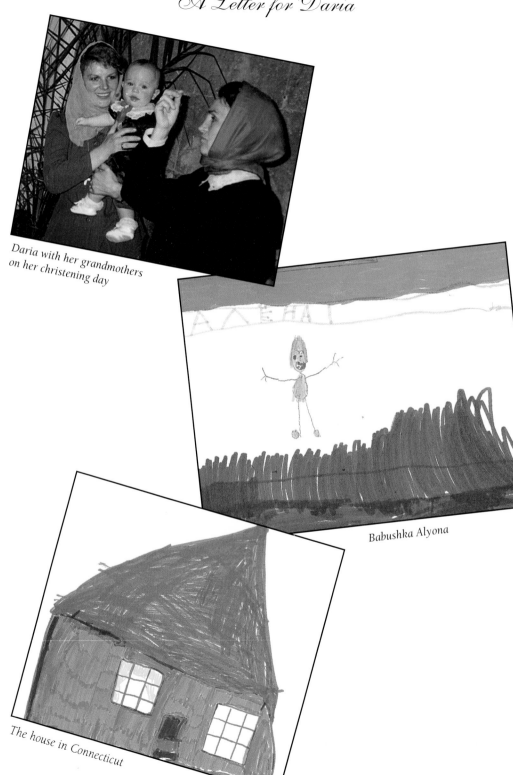

Daria with her grandmothers on her christening day

Babushka Alyona

The house in Connecticut

A Letter for Daria

Daria with her friend Svetlana at the dacha

The dacha

Mama

Daria with her friend Lizzie

SPECIAL THANKS TO:

- Nina Bouis, for understanding the Russian soul and the American work ethic
- Deb Nast, who always understands and supports me
- my loving mom and lovable daughter, without whom this book would never have been written
- my Stars on Ice friends, who are also Daria's friends
- Daria's teacher, Mrs. Cabb, for teaching Daria many important things
- Daria's friends in school, who make her home here in America so special
- all the photographers who graciously allowed the use of their photos
- and all the babushkas of the world